UNDERSTANDING
and standing under
THE
BHAGAVAD GITA

DONALD CURTIS

Science of **Mind** Publishing
Los Angeles, California

UNDERSTANDING

and standing under

THE
BHAGAVAD GITA

Other books by Donald Curtis

Your Thoughts Can Change Your Life

Helping Heaven Happen

The Way of the Christ

New Age Understanding

The Christ-Based Teachings

Happiness and Success Through Personal Power

Master Meditations: A Spiritual Day Book

Daily Power for Joyful Living

Human Problems and How to Solve Them

How to Be Great

Live It Up!

Ten Steps to Personal Power

How to Be Happy and Successful

Love and Marriage

Songs of the Soul

You Are a Wonderful Person

Cosmic Awareness

40 Steps to Self Mastery

Finding the Christ

The Twenty-Third Psalm

To
Casa De Lus

Acknowledgments

My deep gratitude to: Cheryl Lee Kimbo, my literary assistant, for her suggestions, attention to detail, and professional skill in preparing the manuscript; Sandy Sarr, editor of Science of Mind Publishing, for her encouragement and vision in publishing this work; and to Karen Lee Curtis, my life partner and inspiration, for her insights and invaluable assistance with this project.

Donald Curtis

Contents

Foreword

*I*n one of my most recent books, *Your Sacred Self,* I introduced a metaphor adapted from a story told by Henri J.M. Nouwen, which describes the struggle between our ego self and our Sacred Self, and I presented methods by which we can identify and overcome the pull of our destructive ego.

It is not a coincidence that the Bhagavad Gita, an ancient Hindu scripture dating back more than 5,000 years, deals with these same struggles. Truth is the same, no matter where or when or how we find it. What does change is our acknowledgment of the truth, the depth of our understanding of it, and the way in which we choose to apply it in our lives.

Whether we are a psychologist, a storyteller, a Hindu, a spiritual teacher, or a reader, reading this book—we are all on the same human path, working to keep our ego in check and to more fully express our Sacred Self—our "Higher Self," as Donald Curtis puts it—in order to achieve our individual and collective dreams of peace, happiness, health, prosperity, and love.

In the midst of a global spiritual awakening taking place before us, it is important for our Western culture to recognize that the truths we learn here are not any different from those learned by our brothers and sisters living on the Eastern side of our planet. In fact, there are times when a different explanation of the same idea suddenly makes it crystal clear.

In the pages which follow, renowned spiritual teacher Donald Curtis gives us a splendid introduction into this ancient Eastern scripture and its teachings. His simple, direct presentation makes it easy for us to understand, as he shows us how alike we really are in our spiritual teachings and human goals. He explains the meaning of unfamiliar Eastern terms and concepts, and provides comparative excerpts from the Bhagavad Gita and our own Bible, the similarities of which cannot be refuted.

Learning to awaken and express our Sacred Self is humanity's true destiny. Finding new ways to understand the meaning of ourselves allows us to propel forward in this quest. Reading this book and using the meditations in our daily quietude will help us to skip further along on our own Sacred Path of self-fulfillment.

With Love and Light,
Dr. Wayne W. Dyer
Your Sacred Self, Your Erroneous Zones

Preface

*H*ave you ever had the experience of feeling that you knew a great deal about a certain subject, but then in the face of transcendent instruction and revelation, you found with all of your supposed wisdom and understanding you actually knew very little?

This experience is both humbling and inspiring, as I am sure you will agree if it has happened to you. If so, you will be grateful, as I am, that something has revealed new dimensions of spiritual awareness and rescued you from stultifying sameness and ego self-satisfaction.

The first time this happened to me, I was a Religious Science Minister and had been teaching the Science of Mind accredited classes from *The Science of Mind* by Dr. Ernest Holmes, several times a week for more than fifteen years. I was inspired and instructed by this remarkable book and still am, but at that particular time a number of years ago, I felt I had exhausted the resources of the Textbook and expressed as much to a wise teacher, "I don't think I can teach from this book another year."

Very thoughtfully, he replied, "This year, teach between the lines."

This simple statement struck me with the power of lightning. I snatched up my copy of the Textbook and feverishly leafed through the well-worn, familiar pages, aquiver with the excitement of finding new truths and fresh inspiration. I was not disappointed. It was as if I had never read the book before, let alone mastered it and taught it. Everything was fresh and new to me and continues to be so to this day, many years later. All I have to do is "read between the lines."

During many years of spiritual teaching I continue to read between the lines with everything I study and teach. Always, more is being revealed than we are aware of. As a great philosopher said, "My books are both written and unwritten." There is always "the gap"—the space between—where Truth expresses Itself.

"When the pupil is ready the teacher appears." The teacher may come in various guises. It may be as an actual personage—a guru. Or the teacher may be an experience from which we learn. Or it may be a flash of insight, of spiritual awareness, or the revealing of some previously hidden Spiritual Truth which lifts our consciousness to new levels of enlightenment and understanding above anything we have ever known before.

Sometimes the teacher takes the form of a book or scripture which supplies inspiration for progressively unfolding consciousness over continuing periods of time. The bibles of humankind's various spiritual and religious traditions and approaches, including our own Judeo-Christian Bible, are teachers for the faithful who study them and are guided by them. We find a wealth of spiritual instruction when we study the Holy Books of other religions and realize that "Truth is One. The sages call it by many names." These books are teachers which expand our consciousness and lead us ever onward and upward.

For me, the teacher appeared through the Bhagavad Gita. Through the study of this enlightened work, the teacher appears again and again in familiar places where I ceased to be aware of Truth, because I failed to read between the lines. It is important that we do not resist the teachings of other scriptures because their statement is different from our own. On the contrary, this difference of expression may be the exact key we need to unlock the treasures they reveal.

My promise, based upon my own experience, is that you will profit greatly in many ways by a dedicated study of the Bhagavad Gita. Approach it with an open mind, eager to expand the dimensions of your present understanding. There are many translations of the Gita, which was originally written in Sanskrit. Even though you will find the text filled with unfamiliar names and phrases, a simple Hindu glossary will set you on the right track.

I recommend that you acquire a good translation of the Bhagavad Gita as soon as possible.[1] Study it and meditate upon

---

[1]*One of the finest translations for personal study is by Torkom Saraydarian, The Aquarian Educational Group, Sedona, Arizona.*

its various passages. An understanding of the Bhagavad Gita should be sought by all serious spiritual students.

Approach your study with the attitude that you are the pupil who is ready for the teacher (the Bhagavad Gita) to appear. Let the teacher speak to you directly. Listen carefully with your entire being. You will find that spiritual understanding means "standing under God's Law."

This will be confirmed when you are "Understanding and Standing Under the Bhagavad Gita."

UNDERSTANDING
and standing under

THE
BHAGAVAD GITA

Part I

Introduction to the Bhagavad Gita

One of the most fascinating of humanity's spiritual scriptures is the Bhagavad Gita, which means, literally, "the Song of God" and is usually designated as the Hindu Bible. This appellation is not entirely accurate, because even though the Bhagavad Gita is based upon the Vedas and the Upanishads, the most ancient of all recorded spiritual teachings, some of which date back over 5,000 years, the Gita itself is not regarded as scripture actually revealed by God to humankind, but as the teachings of divine incarnations, saints and prophets who interpret and explain the Divine Truths given by God.

If not exactly the Hindu Bible, the Bhagavad Gita is the Gospel of India, the most popular book of Hindu spiritual literature, and it continues to influence the spiritual, cultural, intellectual, and political life of the country just as it has through many centuries.

Mahatma Gandhi, the great Indian leader, was greatly influenced by both the Bhagavad Gita and the Sermon on the Mount. These two texts were his bibles, his guidance on the spiritual path. Gandhi, as did Martin Luther King, Jr., derived his concepts of passive nonresistance, harmlessness (*ahimsa*), peace, and liberation through the realization of the Self from these two sources.

The influence of the Bhagavad Gita continues to be felt upon the entire world, and along with our own Sermon on the Mount, from the teachings of the Christ, will fuse together to form the basis for world brotherhood, world government, and lasting peace.

True spiritual teachers down through the ages have encouraged a scope of spiritual understanding which expands beyond hereditary, cultural, ethnic, and secular denominational boundaries. These teachers always emphasized the unity of Father-Mother God with all people everywhere, expressed through the realization of the Self, the One inherent in all Life. [2]

---

[2] *"God" and the "One" as used in this presentation are synonymous, and refer to the Universal Power, Presence, and Energy which is the Source of all Life. These designations are spiritual, but have no religious connotation.*

This Spiritual Truth is the basis of all religion. Its first expression in the Vedas and Upanishads of India is the Ancient Wisdom inherent in all religions, even though not always clearly understood because of cultural and sectarian differences.

The Bhagavad Gita consists of eighteen chapters compiled from the great Hindu epic poem, "The Mahabharata," which was handed down orally from generation to generation until the Bhagavad Gita was compiled into its present form by Vyasa, a mythical, divine individual, somewhat similar to the way scriptures of other religions have been formulated.

Like the Judeo-Christian Bible and other enlightened spiritual teachings, the Bhagavad Gita is told in parables which reveal great spiritual Truths. The Bhagavad Gita presents the events of a great war between two opposing factions. The setting is the battlefield in the middle of the forest where the conflict is taking place. Two great Rishis (Hindu saints or sages) meet and contemplate the situation unfolding before them. One of the Rishis is the charioteer Arjuna, who has been forced into taking sides in the battle, which entails the necessity of taking up arms against his own kinfolk.

Counseling Arjuna in meeting this difficult challenge is the second Rishi, Krishna. The entire Bhagavad Gita is taken up with the dialogue between these two. Arjuna is the immature, questing individual soul who is seeking Truth, but is enmeshed in world and sensory experience and cannot find his way.

Krishna is Truth. Krishna represents the One—the

Teacher—the Christ within—the Ultimate. Krishna helps Arjuna reach spiritual understanding by answering his questions, thereby guiding him not only to the solution of his current challenge, but also to a complete awareness and understanding of the nature of Life and the way to live it.

The entire event is a parable of the realization of Spirit by the individual. Arjuna is actually the lower self and Krishna is the Higher Self. The lower self is the human ego personality. The Higher Self is our spiritual individuality—our oneness with Spirit. It is our God Self. The war represents the conflict between these two polarities in the human soul. The battlefield is the immediate challenge of everyday experience. Each of us is Arjuna, the seeker, and each of us is Krishna, the Teacher.

This is the meaning of the Bhagavad Gita, told in broad strokes. Krishna instructs Arjuna until the great parable concludes with the enlightenment of Arjuna and the peaceful settlement of the war during which error is slain and Truth is victorious.

The exalted teachings of the Infinite Truths of Ancient Wisdom are presented by Krishna throughout this great spiritual document under the headings of eighteen specific lessons, covering the entire scope of human consciousness as it unfolds from:

Darkness into Light
Ignorance into Enlightenment
Death into Immortality.

The sublime challenge of the Bhagavad Gita moves us into ever ascending awareness of the One—of the First Cause of all manifestation and the Unity behind all Creation. The parable of the Bhagavad Gita concludes with the joyous fusion of Arjuna and Krishna as One. An ever expanding understanding comes to us as we read the lines and between the lines of this great Guide to Life.

A careful comparison of the scriptures of the various religions reveals a unity of agreement which indicates that they all came from the One Source. Careful study readily reveals the common basis of the teachings of the Bhagavad Gita and both our Old and New Testaments, as well as many other world scriptures.

The Bhagavad Gita is a powerful allegorical story of the battle that commences when the lower self is confronted with the knowledge of the Higher Self. The Higher Self within wants to reach down and pull the powerful small ego into the Light, but alas! the small ego perceives this as death.

Taken from an ancient scripture that is classified along with the Vedas and the Upanishads as a spiritual guide, as a bible, the Bhagavad Gita is the epitome of spiritual wisdom and teaches valuable techniques of spiritual living.

The Story

Let us look first of all at the story of the Bhagavad Gita, which tells of a conflict between two branches of one family. We can consider it as an actual human family, or we can consider it as the division that takes place between the "families" existing within each one of us when the Higher Self—the Spiritual Self—becomes involved with our lower mental, emotional, and physical levels. A war is usually taking place between these two levels of the self.

The backdrop of the Bhagavad Gita is a battle where these two factions of the same family are fighting each other for the rights to rule the kingdom. It is a parable for the conflict between the lower self and the Higher Self.

The Conflict

As spiritual teachers point out, the Higher Self is always endeavoring to reach down and bring the lower self up to the realization of its True Nature, but the lower self resists. There is a conflict. There is a battle. The lower self, which we call the little personal ego, or the lesser self, is afraid that if it lets go of its territory or the right to the kingdom established by personality identity rather than individual realization, it will die.

This lower self does not realize that when it follows the guidance of the Higher Self it will be lifted up and transmuted, and there will be peace in the kingdom. The lower self and the Higher Self will become One. The pairs of opposites will be dissolved. As we know from our spiritual lessons and from many teachings of antiquity as well as revelations from the Great Ones, resolving the pairs of opposites is one of the major steps we must take toward spiritual realization.

Krishna and Arjuna

Krishna and Arjuna are two great Rishis living in the forest, contemplating Divine Wisdom. The forest represents our life—our experience. The forest has many trees, great vegetation of dignity and wonder, but we can become lost in the forest if we do not follow the passageways to Light.

Krishna is the Spiritual Self, the Higher Self. Arjuna is the unfolding human soul. Krishna instructs Arjuna, and the entire structure of the Bhagavad Gita is made up of these instructions.

These two Rishis chose the event of war as the background to teach the world the science of liberation and self-realization.

The Battleground

The battleground is our life of daily deeds, emotions, and thoughts. Just as in the Judeo-Christian Bible and other Scriptures, they are told as literal events, but need to be interpreted allegorically, symbolically, and mystically, in order for us to understand the spiritual Truths masked behind the literal account.

We are now embarking upon the battle that is reported in the Bhagavad Gita. We are both Krishna and Arjuna. We are both the teacher and the student. We are both the Christ Self and the unfolding spiritual soul. The two armies represent the energies that fight for the liberation of the human being from the forces of separation and materialization.

Follow this symbolism very carefully. Identify yourself with both Krishna and Arjuna. The battle taking place within us is made up of our energies and the forces these energies generate. In one direction, the Higher Self moves us toward liberation, while in the other direction, the lower self moves us toward separation and the materialization that locks us into form.

Symbolism

Krishna, as the Inner Guide, teaches Arjuna the science of self-realization. The unfolding human soul is represented by Arjuna, who at this stage is confused and torn between his Higher and lower selves. Krishna teaches him how to conquer the "not self," and slowly detach himself from his body and its associations, and to identify himself progressively with his inherent Divinity.

We could think of Krishna as being the Son of God, just as we think of the Christ as being the Son of God—God individualized on earth—the Universal becoming personalized and individualized. In the Bhagavad Gita, Krishna represents this universal principle of love and wisdom. Arjuna is the human soul that is here for the purpose of conscious union with the larger One, but is seemingly separated from It.

The Spiritual Struggle

So Krishna asks Arjuna—you and me—to engage in a spiritual struggle, not a worldly one. We are all taken up most of the time with the comings and goings of our daily occupation, with the needs of just plain existence. Sometimes it's a battle. We may be crushed to earth, but we will rise again if we understand our spiritual nature. Our struggles in life are not really worldly ones, even though they seem to be. They are actually spiritual struggles.

Arjuna is not asked to fight kith and kin, but to fight his own lower self. Even though the Bhagavad Gita seems to tell the story of two branches of one family fighting each other, it actually refers to the Higher Self in opposition to the lower self. The Gita is dramatizing the growth process, which sometimes seems like conflict, but really is a step toward the transmutation of the energies to a higher level of being.

Harmony and Agreement

Many passages in the Bhagavad Gita and the Bible, especially the New Testament, although not exactly parallel, are certainly similar and impart the same instruction. It could hardly be otherwise, since both of these great revelations come from the same Source—Divine Wisdom and Love—from God.

Recognizing both Krishna and the Christ to be the embodiment and the individualization of the One, we understand their teachings to be the same, even though they are stated in the vernacular and tradition of two different cultures. Krishna and the Christ are both the Son of God, who speaks through them.

Truth

Truth is one. We call it by many names. Truth is a synonym for God, and God is all in all. God is all-knowing, all-powerful, and all-present. All of God is present in each one of us. We avail ourselves of all the enlightened teachings and writings of great teachers who have walked among us and have left their heritage of spiritual enlightenment for us to follow in expanding our own consciousness.

One such writing is the Bhagavad Gita, which presents eighteen wonderful lessons that lead us into greater awareness and understanding.

The Eighteen Lessons of the Bhagavad Gita

The following pages give an overview of the basic concepts inherent in the Bhagavad Gita and suggest how they may be integrated into your spiritual understanding to assist in your unfoldment as you travel the path toward enlightenment.

As you study each of the eighteen lessons in the Bhagavad Gita, you will develop a full understanding of its enlightening teaching.

Part II

Yoga

*E*ast or West, we are all aspiring yogis. We are on the evolutionary path of spiritual realization, no matter what religious or spiritual background or practice we choose. We find ourselves involved *in* the world, but something deep within tells us we are not really *of* the world.

This process has been unfolding since the beginning of time. Ancient shamans taught that individual being was a spark from the flame of Infinite Being, which was always striving to unite with its Source. This striving gave rise to spiritual disciplines of worship that lead to union with the One.

As we begin to recognize that all life is spiritual expression, we seek to express the One in all we are and do. This is the practice of yoga. Understanding what yoga is heals separation within ourselves, unifies us with the One, and unites all of us in our mutual pathway toward perfection.

The Bhagavad Gita is actually a book about yoga. "Yoga" means "union," the sum total of all spiritual teaching. The Gita talks about the teaching as being yoga. The one who pursues this teaching and has come to a point of some understanding, proficiency, realization, and development, is a yogi.

There are four basic types of yoga:

1. *Karma Yoga* - Selfless Action in Service
2. *Jnana Yoga* - Knowledge
3. *Bhakti Yoga* - Devotion
4. *Raja Yoga* - Meditation

The first third of the Bhagavad Gita (Lessons 1-6) deals with Karma Yoga (selfless action in service). The middle third (Lessons 7-12) has to do with Jnana Yoga (knowledge or understanding the use of the mind). The final third (Lessons 13-18) pertains to Bhakti Yoga (devotion). Throughout the discourse is Raja Yoga (meditation).

There are other specific classifications of yoga, but they are all under these four areas. In the West, our various types of affirmations, prayers, spiritual mind treatments, and meditations are all forms of yoga. Our way of life, and our religious, cultural, social, and occupational attitudes are all forms of yoga. In other words, these are factors in finding our union with God. Life itself is the ultimate Yoga. Those who are on the Path are yogis.

Customs, habits, and traditions vary between East and West, but the universality of the Bhagavad Gita dissolves all differences, and we are One in its Supernal Light. Similarly, we find our Oneness in the Old Testament Psalms. The Gita and the Psalms are Songs of Life whose melodies flow through our souls and through our entire being.

Karma Yoga—Selfless Action in Service

We set the great Law of Cause and Effect in action by everything we do. Our karma is the accumulation in our consciousness resulting from cause and effect activities and our attitudes toward them. We build constructive karma when we engage in beneficial activities and when our attitude is selfless and dedicated to service.

The Law of Karma (cause and effect) works identically for everyone. It is universal. It has nothing to do with East or West, or with religious, social, or cultural factors. The Law of Cause and Effect (Karma) works the same for all.

Selfless action is attained when a person detaches from concern regarding results and does what has to be done, simply because it is necessary to do so. Action is the process of expressing Spirit. There is a razor's edge of difference between action and nonaction. Action is contained in nonaction, and nonaction in action. Understanding Karma Yoga inspires us to live a life of dedicated service.

Selfish action is the attitude which asks, "What's in it for me?" For instance, people who give their tithe only because they expect to receive are indulging in selfish action. Persons who give with no thought of return are performing selfless action. Selfless actions build constructive (good) karma. Selfish action does the opposite.

A Rosicrucian axiom says, "Loving, self-forgetting service is the shortest, the safest, the surest road to God." The Christ directs, *"Let your light so shine before men, that they may see your good works, and glorify your Father which is in Heaven."* (Matthew 5:16)

Jnana Yoga—Knowledge

Knowledge is power. Whatever we know (have knowledge of) appears in our life. Our thoughts and ideas are acted upon by our mind, consciously and subconsciously, bringing them into manifestation. At the superconscious level, we have the capacity to know God. Jnana Yoga assists us in this knowing through techniques of awareness, perception, insight, vision, and attunement. As we practice the Presence, we know that Father-Mother God is everywhere. There is nowhere that God leaves off and we begin. Individually, we realize, "God is all of me. I am that part of God which I can understand." Understanding comes from knowing. Understanding is "standing under" God's Law, which is total Knowledge.

As we turn our thoughts inward and upward toward God, we come to know God. The more we know, the more there is to know. Our thoughts and our feelings join together in conviction, strengthening into an undeviating faith which knows that God is all there is to know. This is followed by the realization that there is no end to that which there is to know. Therefore, we dedicate our life to the Path of Knowledge (Jnana Yoga), recognizing that it is Infinite and Eternal.

Bhakti Yoga—Devotion

The God Chant

Oh my God, my God!
How I love Thee! How I love Thee! How I love Thee!
Oh my God, my God!

How I love Thee! How I love Thee!
My God!

God! God! God!
How I love Thee! How I love Thee! How I love Thee!
God! God! God!
How I love Thee! How I love Thee!
My God!

—*St. Germaine*

St. Augustine prayed, "Father-Mother God, thou has created us for Thyself, and our hearts are ever restless until they return to Thee."

Both of these familiar prayers carry the powerful love and devotion of the individual who lives in God and is totally committed and wholly devoted to the Father-Mother Reality of the One. In practicing Bhakti Yoga (True Devotion) the devotee spends every moment, waking and asleep, experiencing God.

The Bhakti yogi lives and moves and has his or her being in Father-Mother God. Every thought and action is centered in the One. The yogi sees God everywhere and experiences the Infinite One in everything. The Bhakti yogi lives for, with, and in God. This loving devotion to the One is inherent in everyone, and the more devoted we are, the more devoted we become until we are totally absorbed in the One.

The Bhagavad Gita is a celestial song of devotion to the One.

In the West, the Lord's Prayer and the Twenty-third Psalm are transcendent statements of recognition and devotion to the Lord—Father-Mother God—the One.

The Christ Prayer is a declaration of devotion to the One through the Christ:

> *Oh Christ!*
> *Thou Son of God!*
> *My own eternal Self!*
> *Live Thou thy Life in me,*
> *Do Thou thy Will in me,*
> *Be Thou made flesh in me!*
> *I have no will but Thine,*
> *I have no self but Thee,*
> *Oh Christ!*
> *Thou Son of God!*

True devotion is total absorption in the One.

Raja Yoga—Meditation

The difference in the practice of religion in the West and in the East, especially in India, is a matter of degree of intensity. In the Western world, religion is a way of life. In India, religion is life; life is religion. Its practice varies all the way from elaborate formalism and traditionalism to simple devotion and asceticism.

Meditation has always been known and practiced by the mystics of all religions, but the West has never embraced it and practiced it with the focus and discipline of the Eastern devotees of certain schools of Buddhism, Zen, Tao, many branches of Hinduism, and the ubiquitous gurus and holy men of India. In various degrees, meditation is the practice of religion. For many, there is no religion without meditation. For many more, meditation is religion itself. Meditation is more than a process or a technique. Meditation is the spiritual bread of life.

Meditation is the inner experience of the Ultimate Reality. By stilling the senses and quieting the mind and the emotions, the yogi enters a realm of unobstructed silence and neutrality where the world ceases to exist and all things are made new.

In India, meditation starts before birth and continues beyond death. Meditation is the conscious experience of Eternal Life. The meditative approach is inherent in the Indian culture, and in a very real sense, the entire Bhagavad Gita is a meditation. Its great inspiration and power are realized only when approached in this way.

The multitudinous yogis of India are primarily meditators and teachers of meditation. Many have been instrumental in bringing meditation to acceptance in the West. Meditation training and practice is an important part of the modern spiritual approaches of metaphysics, mysticism, and various New Thought and New Age schools and centers, as well as various esoteric and occult teachings. Meditation is also taught and practiced now in many orthodox churches, after having been ignored and resisted for hundreds of years, even though meditation is taught throughout the Bible, in both the Old and New Testaments.

Part III

Health and Healing in the Bhagavad Gita

"To heal" means "to make whole." The entire theme of the Bhagavad Gita is wholeness—Oneness. In explaining the perfect nature of the One, Krishna shows us that when we recognize and experience our Oneness with the One, we are whole as It is whole. That is, we are spiritual beings going through a human experience. Our sustained health and healing depend upon identifying ourselves with our spiritual nature rather than our human experience.

Modern science has proven that preventative medicine is more effective than corrective or emergency measures. The

Bhagavad Gita tells us our health and healing come from identifying ourselves with the One which is perfect. When we experience a sense of separation from the One, illness and disease set in. Only when we return in consciousness to the Source are we healed. It is therefore obvious that Spirit is the original preventative medicine and the ultimate healing therapy.

Modern metaphysical and spiritual mind healing techniques are based upon the recognition of God as the One First Cause. The entire Bhagavad Gita is a thrilling exposition of this principle, establishing the standard of consciousness which we must attain if we are to experience wholeness. When we sustain a high spiritual consciousness of Oneness with God, no further healing is necessary; this Unification is the healing. But if we are deficient in spiritual consciousness, then our human errors must be corrected before we can be healed.

There is nothing new in these principles concerning causation and healing, and the part our consciousness plays in the process. These principles are taught and practiced in both the Old and the New Testaments. Modern psychology and psychotherapy as well as metaphysical and spiritual mental healing practices are based upon them.

These teachings were set forth thousands of years ago in India and also appear in other early teachings, including those from ancient Egypt, Greece, and the Orient.

The Bhagavad Gita reiterates over and over that consciousness is cause. Human consciousness must be attuned to God consciousness if humanity is to express its divinity. The Bhagavad Gita is an absolute spiritual teaching interspersed with specific concrete guidelines we must follow to reach spiritual realization, which is the true healing.

Healing Passages from the Bhagavad Gita

The Real

> *Know that the Real is indestructible. No one can destroy the immutable Being pervaded by the imperishable One. (Bhagavad Gita 2:17)*

When we have a full understanding of the nature of Being, we cannot help but realize there is never anything to be healed. The Real is indestructible and imperishable. In healing we need only to free ourselves from the unreal—the illusion—and reveal the Real. This is the process of healing. The revealing of the Real is the healing.

Purity

Be firmly fixed in purity, free from all thoughts of acquisition and attachment, and be established in the Self. (Bhagavad Gita 2:45)

The Bhagavad Gita consistently points out that the cause of all indisposition is negative consciousness. Freedom from negation is best achieved by not allowing it to become established in the first place. Negation cannot enter our consciousness when it is already filled with purity and identified with the Self.

Dominion

The Supreme Self of one who has attained self-control and is balanced and serene, is balanced in cold and heat, pleasure and pain, honor and dishonor. (Bhagavad Gita 6:7)

Personal dominion over one's mind is the only dependable basis for health and wholeness. The Supreme Self of our being is permanently established within us as eternal potential, but it is conditioned by our human consciousness and is limited by it. When we are balanced and serene, the human self becomes one with the Supreme Self.

Yoga

> *Yoga destroys pain and sorrow in one who is temperate in eating and recreation, who is moderate in action, and who is regulated in sleep and wakefulness.(Bhagavad Gita 6:17)*

Yoga means union—integration—oneness. When true yoga is attained, everything counter to the inner state of union with the One is dissolved and healing can take place. Personal discipline in regulating habits and establishing a constructive lifestyle is essential in attaining yoga. Yoga is health. Yoga is healing.

The Source

> *I am the Source of all. From Me all of creation evolves. The wise worship Me with loving consciousness of conviction. (Bhagavad Gita 10:8)*

There is One Perfect Life. This Life is our life now. This One is the Source from which all creation flows. Every cell, every vibration of our bodies, and every nuance of our thoughts and feelings have their perfect pattern in this One Source. This is our health. Remembering this in times of challenge is our healing.

Worship

He who is devoted to Me, who looks upon Me as the Supreme, free from attachment and enmity toward all, comes to Me in his worship. (Bhagavad Gita 11:55)

Worship is the process of attuning the individual to the Universal. Devotion and reverence for the Supreme bring health to the consciousness of the worshiper. "To worship" means "to make worthy." This cannot be accomplished when the individual is attached to externals or has any feeling but love for others. Attachment and hatred cause disease. Worship in love heals.

Balance

He who has no ill will, who is friendly and compassionate, free from egoism and attachment, balanced in pleasure and pain, forgiving, ever content, self-controlled, possessed of firm conviction, with mind and understanding dedicated to Me, this devotee is dear to Me. (Bhagavad Gita 12:13,14)

Health and healing result from the balance which is brought about by dissolving the pairs of opposites. This is a form of the healing technique of denials and affirmation, whereby we remove all belief in negative false concepts and firmly establish faith in constructive belief. When the individual accomplishes this, healing is the result: "This devotee is dear to Me."

Liberation

He who serves Me with unfailing devotion, transcends the gunas,³ and is fit for liberation. (Bhagavad Gita 14:26)

This is a counterpart to the statement of the Christ: "In the world you have tribulation, but be of good cheer. I have overcome the world." The world is limited by the gunas, which are the qualities and substances of Nature, but our consciousness is unlimited when we are centered in the One. Our liberation—our healing—is accomplished in the Spirit.

Freedom

Our Divine Nature leads to freedom; our lower nature leads to bondage. (Bhagavad Gita 16:5)

³*Gunas (levels of consciousness). See Part VI.*

The healing message here is crystal clear. "Bondage" is problem, disease, difficulty. The cause of these comes from our lower nature—our false beliefs, negativity, and human limitation. Our thinking must be brought in line with our Divine Nature—the perfection of God within us, the Source from which all blessings flow. Our freedom is the result of having perfect health and demonstrating complete healing.

Transmutation

He who is free from attachment and desire, and has subdued his lower self, attains the state of freedom and transcendence. (Bhagavad Gita 18:49)

The Bhagavad Gita stresses throughout that we are in a state of limitation and disease when we are contaminated with attachment and desire. These are of the lower self and are the root of all suffering. This suffering takes many forms and will continue until the energies of the lower self are transmuted into the Higher Self, and our consciousness is raised. Health and healing are the result.

Serenity

Abandoning egoism, force, arrogance, desire, anger and self-aggrandizement, and becoming serene in mind, the individual enters into the Eternal One. (Bhagavad Gita 18:53)

There is no law of error and disease. They are the misbegotten progeny of human thinking that has become distorted by negativity, false beliefs, and separation from the One. When we recognize the personal faults and bad habits which limit, weaken, and sicken us, we can take steps to eliminate them. When this healing process is accomplished, we attain perfect health.

Part IV

The Bhagavad Gita and the Bible

*M*any passages in the Bhagavad Gita and the Bible, especially in the New Testament, although not exactly parallel, are certainly similar and impart the same instruction. It could hardly be otherwise, since both of these great spiritual guidebooks come from the same Source—Divine Wisdom and Love—God.

Both Krishna and the Christ are the embodiment and the individualization of the One. The teachings are the same, even though stated in the vernacular and tradition of two different cultures. Note the similarity of the following passages:

Oneness

Both scriptures emphasize our Oneness with God. There is no place where God leaves off and we begin. We are all individualizations of the One. Father-Mother God is the parentage of each one of us. We are all made in the image and likeness of God; therefore, "God is the same in all." God must always come first. This unifies and strengthens us.

The Bhagavad Gita says:

Unity of mind overcomes the world. God is the same in all. (Bhagavad Gita 5:19)

From the Bible:

I and my Father are one. (John 10:30)
He that hath seen me hath seen the Father. (John 14:9)
And I, if I be lifted up from the earth, will draw all men unto me. (John 12:32)

The First Commandment says:

I am the Lord thy God... Thou shalt have no other Gods before me. (Exodus 20: 2, 3)

These supernal ideas expand our consciousness. God expresses through us. "A mind expanded to the dimensions of a greater idea can never return to its original size." The Bhagavad Gita and the Bible are filled with greater ideas. As we meditate upon the great Truths we are lifted to new levels of understanding.

Freedom

We are told that knowing the Truth sets us free. When liberation is our goal, we establish dominion over our minds by dissolving desire, fear, and anger. This enables us to receive the riches of the kingdom which the Father joyously gives us.

From the Bhagavad Gita:

Self-controlled souls who are free from anger and desire, who control the mind, and have realized the Self, find absolute freedom. (Bhagavad Gita 5:26)
When the senses and the mind are controlled, when desire, fear, and anger are cast away, and liberation is the supreme goal, the sage attains complete freedom. (Bhagavad Gita 5:28)

From the Bible:

Your Father knoweth what things ye have need of, before ye ask him.
(Matthew 6:8)
It is the Father's good pleasure to give you the kingdom. (Luke
12:32)

Why should there be stress and strain? There is no reason to toil and endure needless, unnecessary suffering, when we can go to the center and find there our Oneness with the One, and find peaceful, blissful unfoldment of our lives. As we practice meditation, we learn how to be still and know that the presence within is God.

In the Bhagavad Gita, Krishna, the Higher Self, is teaching Arjuna, our soul, which is continuing to grow. Krishna is the Teacher; Arjuna is the chelah (disciple or follower). As has been previously mentioned, the setting is a battlefield, which is symbolic of the fact that our Higher Self and our lower self are often in conflict with each other. The two together are building our consciousness.

When our little self, Arjuna, our younger, personal ego self, is in charge, we are often upset by the things that take place in the world. But when we align ourselves totally with the Higher Self, we are lifted up from this world, and we are drawn unto a higher level. The battle is not an external battle at all; it is an inner one.

Forgiveness

Seeing God in each other is one of the most important steps of spiritual growth. All of us are children of God, therefore we are one with each other. No one is better than anyone else. We are all superior when we have the same regard for everyone.

He who has the same regard for friends, companions, foes, the neutral, the hateful, relatives, the righteous and the unrighteous, is a superior person. (Bhagavad Gita 6:9)

Love your enemies, bless them that curse you, do good to them that hate you, and pray for them which despitefully use you, and persecute you. (Matthew 5:44)

This is the way to liberation. This is the way to freedom. This is the way to Light. "To forgive" means "to give for." We must learn to give for our feelings of discrimination, animosity, and judgment, feelings of love, blessing, and empathy. There can be no compromise with principle. No deviation is allowed.

Love and equal-mindedness are equated as our only acceptable attitudes toward each other. The ability to act with equanimity rather than animosity is the mark of a superior person. Each of us has the capacity to reach the level of consciousness where we are in control of our feelings and actions, and have dominion over all relationships.

Meditation

Both scriptures emphasize the importance of meditation, based upon solitude and quietude. Poised and centered in spiritual consciousness, the mind becomes steady, balanced, and controlled, with single focus upon the One.

From the Bhagavad Gita:

Let the yogi constantly keep the mind steady, remaining in solitude, with the mind and body controlled, free from desire and greed. (Bhagavad Gita 6:10)
The yogi, always keeping the mind balanced and controlled, attains peace and liberation, and abides in Me. (Bhagavad Gita 6:15)

From the Bible:

Be still, and know that I am God. (Psalm 46:10)
The light of the body is the eye: if therefore thine eye be single, thy whole body shall be full of light. (Matthew 6:22)

Let the light come into your consciousness. When we meditate, the "I"—the "eye"—becomes single.

Whenever there is outer turbulence, be still and know that the Presence within is God. God is our Real Self. The yogi is one who is unified with the Truth. Yoga is Oneness. A yogi is one who practices Oneness. We are all yogis when we are unified with spiritual Truth. Yoga itself is the science of the Spirit.

The instruction from the Bhagavad Gita and from the Bible helps us raise our consciousness to higher levels.

God, the One

Superior and eternal, the One is the highest and most valuable of all creation. Magnificent and brilliant, God transcends everything and is the only One.

From the Bhagavad Gita:

There is nothing higher than I. All that is, is strung on Me as clusters of gems on a string. (Bhagavad Gita 7:7)
I am the eternal seed of all beings. I am the intelligence of the intelligent. I am the splendour of the splendid. (Bhagavad Gita 7:10)

From the Bible:

Even from everlasting to everlasting, thou art God. (Psalm 90:2)
Hear, O Israel, The Lord our God is one Lord. (Deuteronomy 6:4)

As we experience God's Presence within us at all times, there is no difference between the Real Self and our own Higher Self. As we know that "from everlasting unto everlasting," the God Presence is within us, we are lifted up to expanded realization on all levels.

Knowledge and Wisdom

As we evolve upward along the pathway to perfection, we seek to become virtuous and devout. Our worship is raising our consciousness to the One.

> *The virtuous ones who worship Me are of four kinds: the one in distress, the seeker of knowledge, the seeker for wealth, and the one aspiring to wisdom. Of these, the wise ones who are ever steadfast and devoted to the One, are most dear to Me. (Bhagavad Gita 7:16, 17)*

> *Get wisdom; and with all thy getting, get understanding. (Proverbs 4:7)*

Wisdom is the balance and equilibrium that comes from experience, from instruction, and from spiritual realization. These give us wisdom. After wisdom comes understanding.

Understanding is standing under God's law—standing under the realization of the overall canopy of Light, Love, and Truth. So get wisdom. Knowledge comes first, and knowing how to relate to ourself, to God, and to our world. This gives us understanding. Stand upon the Truth. Stand under the Law and the Presence of God.

The Eternal

Brahman is the One. Brahman is God. Krishna, in the Bhagavad Gita, is the Voice of God—the Presence of God. The name "Krishna" is very similar to the name "Christ." Each is the Son of God. Krishna is the Christ of Brahman, the Higher Self, the Son of God, the True Teacher.

> *The objective basis of all created things is the perishable nature; and the essence of the indwelling divine elements is the subjective phenomenon of existence. (Bhagavad Gita, 8:4)*

The perishable nature, the objective, is always the outer. So the objective phenomenon, the things that we see in the outer world, are the ones that we respond to with our five senses. The subjective is inner. Subjective phenomena include love, peace, truth, harmony, intuition, awareness, inspiration, and all spiritual qualities. These are the aspects of our consciousness.

Neither shall they say, Lo here! or Lo there! for behold, the Kingdom of God is within you. (Luke 17:21)

Both the Bhagavad Gita and the Sermon on the Mount tell us to release the outer and find our real life in the inner. The keys to the kingdom are in both; they confirm that the kingdom of God is within us, and then agree with Jesus when he teaches:

Judge not according to the appearance, but judge righteous judgment. (John 7:24)

The appearances are what we respond to with our five senses, but back of the appearance is the cause. When we know the Truth, we will be One with the One First Cause.

From the Bhagavad Gita:

Remember Me at all times. When your mind and understanding are fixed on Me, you will surely come to Me alone. (Bhagavad Gita 8:7)

From the Bible:

I and my Father are one. (John 10:30)

He that hath seen me hath seen the Father. (John 14:9)
Draw nigh to God, and he will draw nigh to you. (James 4:8)

Both scriptures not only emphasize the essential spiritual requirements of reaching the realization of Oneness, but they also tell us how this realization is to be attained—through focus and direction.

Most Profound Knowledge

The ultimate supernal knowledge is to know that in God we live and move and have our being, and to know that God knows our needs and provides whatever we have need of.

Behold My divine mystery. Beings do not dwell in Me. My Spirit which is the Source of all beings sustains the beings but does not abide in them. As the mighty wind, moving everywhere, rests always in space, in the same manner all beings abide in Me. (Bhagavad Gita 9:5, 6)

Nothing illustrates these teachings more clearly and vividly than this passage from the Bible in the Sermon on the Mount:

Consider the lilies of the field, how they grow; they toil not, neither

do they spin: And yet I say unto you, That even Solomon in all
his glory was not arrayed like one of these. (Matthew 6:28, 29)
Wherefore, if God so clothe the grass of the field, which to day is,
and to morrow is cast into the oven, shall he not much more
clothe you, O ye of little faith? (Matthew 6:30)
Therefore take no thought, saying, What shall we eat? or, What
shall we drink? or, Wherewithal shall we be clothed? (For after all
these things do the Gentiles seek:) for your heavenly Father
knoweth that ye have need of all these things. (Matthew 6:31, 32)
But seek ye first the kingdom of God, and his righteousness; and
all these things shall be added unto you. (Matthew 6:33)

Repeated over and over, the basic theme in both the Bible
and the Bhagavad Gita is: "I and my Father are One." Both the
Bhagavad Gita and the Bible give us instruction about how to
live, and how to relate to ourselves, to God, and to each other.

Yoga of Devotion

Friendliness, compassion, and love lift us out of our egotistical
consciousness and attachment to things, and inspire us in our
devotion to the One.

From the Bhagavad Gita:

He who has no ill will, is friendly and compassionate to all, who is free from attachment and egoism, balanced in pleasure and in pain, patient, ever content and self-controlled, with firm conviction, and with mind and understanding dedicated to Me, this devotee is dear to Me. (Bhagavad Gita 12:14)

From the Bible:

This is my commandment. That ye love one another. (John 15:12)
Go and sell that thou hast, give to the poor...and come and follow me. (Matthew 19:21)

Give up poor things. Give up the little petty personality—the little, shrunken, midget ego stuff, and follow the One. As we follow Him, we are led into those "paths of righteousness" we are told about in the twenty-third Psalm. By taking these paths, we reach a state of inner peace, along with Paul, the great Apostle, who said:

I have learned, in whatsoever state I am, therewith to be content. (Philippians 4:11)

Of all the gifts that God has given us, contentment and peace head the list. The Bible says:

Peace I leave with you, my peace I give unto you: not as the world giveth, give I unto you. Let not your heart be troubled, neither let it be afraid. (John 14:27)
Ye believe in God, believe also in me. (John 14:1)
The peace of God, which passeth all understanding, shall keep your hearts and minds through Jesus Christ. (Philippians 4:7)

The Bhagavad Gita reiterates over and over that there is no higher purpose in life than devotion to God. We are in His favor when we are devoted to Him. Peace beyond comprehension comes to those who come to the One through Krishna, and to God through Christ. Comparing the two scriptures shows us that they are the same.

Yoga of the Supreme Spirit

As we dwell in the consciousness of the Higher Self, we are freed from pride, attachment, and bondage. Delusions are dissolved in the Light of Truth and dwell eternally in the Heavenly Abode.

Free from pride and delusion, victorious over the evil of attachment, dwelling constantly in the Self, their desires having been completely dissolved and freed from the pairs-of-opposites—the undeluded reach the Goal Eternal. That is My Supreme Abode, hidden from sun, moon, and fire. Those who reach it never return. (Bhagavad Gita 15:5, 6)

The Bible tells of how Herod sent the Wise Men to find out where the Christ was to be born (Matthew 3:8). In their contact with the Christ, the Wise Men became Christed, which is what happens to us in our contact with the One, with the Light within. The Light transforms us. In this story the Wise Men were lifted up and transformed by the birth of the Christ, and when the time came to return to their homes, the Bible says:

They departed into their own country another way. (Matthew 3:12)

The Bible and the Bhagavad Gita show us the Way, the Truth, and the Life. Krishna points out to Arjuna in the Bhagavad Gita, "I am the Way. Follow Me." The Christ says:

I am the way, the truth and the life: no man cometh unto the Father, but by me. (John 14:6)
No man can come to me, except the Father which hath sent me draw him. (John 6:44)

Both scriptures confirm that God's Way is the only Way. There is no other path from which to achieve realization of our true, spiritual self. We are One with God in Spirit. God is Spirit. We are spiritual beings, evolving in the Way of Spirit.

Grace

In this state of attunement and alignment, we come to the great concept that is brought out in all spiritual teaching, including these two (the Bhagavad Gita and the Bible)—the state of Grace.

In the Bhagavad Gita, Krishna graphically describes the individual who has attained a state of Grace:

Casting aside self-sense, force, arrogance, desire, anger, possession, egoless and tranquil in mind, he becomes worthy of becoming one with Brahman. (Bhagavad Gita 18:53)

Having become one with Brahman, and being tranquil in spirit, he neither grieves nor desires. Regarding all beings as alike he attains supreme devotion to Me. (Bhagavad Gita 18:54)

Through devotion he comes to know Me, what My measure is and who I am in truth; then, having known Me in truth, he forthwith enters into Me. (Bhagavad Gita 18:55)

Doing continually all actions whatsoever, taking refuge in Me, he reaches by My grace the eternal, undying abode. (Bhagavad Gita 18:56)

Paul, in the Bible, was able to perceive this state very closely when the Lord said unto him:

My grace is sufficient for thee. (I Corinthians 12:9)

Grace is the impersonal outpouring of God's Life into our being. That is all there is to know and all you need to know to follow the Way—the Path of Light. It moves ever onward, ever upward. God's center is everywhere; His circumference is nowhere. The bottom line of all Spiritual Truth has not yet been written.

True Grace has not yet been achieved, but we keep moving on, spiraling up the mountain toward the summit where the One is waiting to greet us, envelop us in Its Entire Being, and bring us into the state of constant Inner Knowing—of Grace, Peace, and Love.

The statements of the Bible and the Bhagavad Gita reinforce each other with subtle nuances of meaning.

Quietude

From an old hymn:

Blessed quietness, holy quietness,

What assurance in my soul,
On the stormy sea,
Speaking peace to me,
How the billows cease to roll.

Both scriptures emphasize the necessity of inner quietude as a prerequisite for experiencing the God state.

Try constantly to keep the mind steady, remain in solitude, with mind and body free from desires and possessions. (Bhagavad Gita 6:10)

Be still and know that I am God. (Psalms 46:10)

We learn to affirm: "I am poised and centered in the Christ Consciousness, and nothing can disturb the calm serenity of my soul." An Oriental aphorism states, "All things proceed from the quiet mind." Calm, quiet, peace, silence, are progressive stages of arriving at that inner state which we designate as "The Silence."

Both the Bible and the Bhagavad Gita state the value of centering the mind in the inner subjective realm and freeing it from all objective, external concerns. The principle is one of release—of letting go and letting God fill our entire being. The instruction assures us that we can reach that silent state by disciplining the conscious mind to free itself from desire and possessions in recognizing its divinity.

Studying the Two Bibles

These are a selected few similar passages from two great master-pieces of spiritual literature—the bibles of both the Eastern and Western statements of Truth. The objectives are the same: to bring a realization of the Nature of God—the One; and to give the instruction which will enable us to win the battle between our lower and higher natures, and thereby to attain our Oneness with God.

Both the Bible and the Bhagavad Gita are infinite wellsprings for inspiration, study, and enlightenment. Both offer great scope for interpretation. They are both rich in symbolism and constantly lead one into greater understanding and eventual enlightenment.

Studying the Bhagavad Gita and the Bible together expands our consciousness and whets our appetite for more and more Truth. These two collections of Supernal Light reinforce each other. They are both gifts from the One.

Part V

Daily Meditations with the Bhagavad Gita

A continuous realization of the Divine Presence is the pivotal element in experiencing the kind of life we desire. When we consistently envelop ourself in a spiritual atmosphere, we align our inner being with right action. Fulfillment, joy, peace, and abundance are available to us when we consciously embrace these ideas, constructively directing our thoughts. These daily meditations help us do this.

The scriptural quotations for these Daily Meditations are from the Bhagavad Gita, and are a composite of many different translations. Numerals in parentheses represent chapter and verse. All editions of the Bhagavad Gita are numbered the same.

How to Use the Meditations

Devote at least fifteen minutes, preferably when you are alone and in a quiet place, to a meditation each day. Read the message for content, simply being aware of the idea it expresses. Then study it more deeply, allowing your thinking to be challenged, stimulated, or enhanced. Finally, to incorporate that idea in your own life, study the affirmation at the end of each meditation. Close your eyes, meditate deeply on its meaning, and let it become a part of you.

■

The Self Is Eternal

The Self is never born, nor does It ever die. Having once come to be, It will not cease to be. The Self is unborn, eternal, changeless, and primeval. It is not slain when the body is killed. (Bhagavad Gita 2:20)

This is a key concept of the Spiritual Truths of the Ancient Wisdom revealed throughout the Bhagavad Gita. Along with other Spiritual Truths, it is repeated over and over again in various guises—psychological, mental, emotional, or literal—because we have these levels within ourselves and they must all be convinced. They must all come to the spiritual realization of Truth.

The customs and traditions of our religions are not all superstitions. If we, in our belief or our faith (belief is a precursor to faith), strive to please God and know we can depend upon God, we will realize that God gives us what we need—protecting our bodies, our homes, our loved ones, our pets, and our world. Some people think we are praying to an outside being and regard it as superstitious. If we truly understand this teaching of the Gita, we see that it is not a superstition.

The scope of the Bhagavad Gita is so extensive that we could spend forever endeavoring to encompass it. So we take a bit at a time and work toward understanding and realization as we go along. We can contemplate the great ideas which the Gita brings forth, selecting passages from the Gita each day and meditating upon them. The understanding will come.

Life is in full, free flow through me. I am a channel through which Eternal Life expresses. I live forever.

■

Involution and Evolution

All beings are unmanifest in the beginning, manifest in the middle, and unmanifest again in the end. What then is there to grieve about? (Bhagavad Gita 2:20)

Krishna poses this question to the entire human family. This passage states the principle of involution and evolution: as the Spirit descends into form, It is locked into that form during its medial experience, then goes back to the unmanifested state through the process of evolution.

All beings were originally in a state of unmanifestation. This is Spirit—unformed, ephemeral, ethereal. Our Spirit is in that state at the beginning. At the midcourse, as It is involuted, It descends into substance, matter, and form. It becomes manifest. This is the middle state.

Now, the undeveloped and the unevolved consciousness believes that this middle stage—manifestation—is the final stage, but it is only the middle stage. This is why Krishna needs to instruct the Arjuna of our understanding—to help us see that the form or the middle stage, even though it is tangible and real in appearance, is not real in the sense of Eternal Reality.

The third stage of evolutionary unfoldment is freeing ourselves from form, freeing ourselves from the negativity and all the attendant challenges of being manifest—then moving into the unmanifest state again, where the cycle repeats itself.

*I am a product of the evolutionary process of involution and evolution.
I express through form, but I am free from it.*

■

Self-Realization

*In the path of the wisdom of Self-realization no effort is ever lost.
Even a little of this knowledge and the practice of spiritual disciplines, protects one from fears. (Bhagavad Gita 2:40)*

This passage covers every contingency, every question that the
seeking soul could possibly have. Throughout the entire
Bhagavad Gita, Arjuna—who represents the lower self, the
ego-self, the struggling soul—is always asking questions.
Krishna answers that if he, and we, are patient enough, the
answers will come.

Sometimes we find challenges in undertaking the spiritual
disciplines of prayer, meditation, right living, and positive
thought. We say, "I just don't think I am getting anywhere. I try
so hard! I reached realization last night in my meditation, but
today everything falls apart."

In our undeveloped Arjuna-state, when we are locked into
feelings that have to do with self-esteem, achievement, and striv-

ing toward perfection, we tend to become discouraged and to condemn ourselves. We create some problem, big or small, that must be met, and we say, "Surely I am a terrible person. I am not getting anywhere spiritually."

The Gita says that is not the case. The point is to keep on keeping on. Keep moving up the mountain, for even though we fail, we do not create contrary results. The important thing is our motivation. We need to keep moving upward. As we pursue the pathway we come to a realization that brings an awareness of a new dimension, a new perspective, and we see— among other things—that birth and death are but experiences as life unfolds.

I anticipate all impending events with enthusiasm and expectation of good. Ease, order, and right action prevail in my life.

■

Contemplation and Action

There are two paths of spiritual realization: the path of knowledge for those of a contemplative nature; and the path of service and action for those given to action. (Bhagavad Gita 3:3)

We are already familiar with these two paths, because both of them are working in each one of us: the path towards spiritual realization through knowledge of the self (for which meditation is the major technique) or the path leading to service in action (for those born to action).

In this chapter, Krishna expounds upon these two different paths. They are not mutually exclusive. They are both pathways up the mountain. We do not attain freedom from action without being active. Also, we do not reach perfection by being nonactive. Paradoxes and apparent contradictions may appear within these lessons, but that does not invalidate them. Such things always appear in the spiritual study, because we are not talking in terms of comparative truth, but rather in terms of Truth which rises above the pairs of opposites.

"Meditate on Me as the One." That is the key. It is not that the One is "out there" and we are "here," and we ask it to come down and help us. Rather, the One is everywhere, known to "those who meditate on me as the One and worship Me in all beings."

Through knowledge of the Self attained by practicing meditation, I contemplate the One and also follow the path of service and action.

■

Freedom from Attachment

Other than work done as and for a sacrifice, the world is bound by action. Perform your work as a sacrifice, free from attachment. (Bhagavad Gita 3:9)

We come here to a concept with which we are familiar, but may not fully understand.

What is Karma? "Man is bound by the fetters of Karma." Karma is the law of cause and effect, of action and reaction. It's as simple as that, but Karma extends over the entire scope of our being, and encompasses and includes all of the lifetimes of the past, including the one we are living now, and will be a factor in the ones which are to come. There is only one continuous lifetime, though we are bound at the Arjuna level by the fetters of Karma.

We must perform our actions as a sacrifice, though we must get the real meaning of sacrifice, thinking of it as an offering of worship. The total and ultimate sacrifice is in the giving of ourselves joyously, in action, to meet the situations of life.

There are many similarities between the Sermon on the Mount and the Bhagavad Gita, because they come from the same Source. There is only One Source—the Ultimate—Eternal Life—Infinite Intelligence—One Mind—the Solar Logos. "Praise God from whom all blessings flow." The Scriptures and the Great Teachings and the Great Truths are restatements in different cultures, historical periods, and degrees and levels of enlightenment, by the seers and the avatars as they teach the Eternal Truth—the Ancient Wisdom—over and over again.

I am free from the bondage of attachment as I fulfill all duties and obligations, as all of my actions express the Truth.

■

Nonattachment

Always perform the work that has to be done without attachment, for by performing action without attachment, man attains the Supreme. (Bhagavad Gita 3:19)

Nonattachment is one of the hardest of lessons. That is why the Bhagavad Gita presents the parable of the battle that ensues when we become attached to ourselves. Arjuna is bogged down here at the soul level by his appetites, his urges, his desires, his possessions.

You and I become attached to the nature of our own personality. We become attached to those close to us, and rightly so, because this is part of our experience of learning to love. We learn to love someone dearly, our sweetheart, our mate, our husband, our wife, our children, our relatives. This is why

Arjuna is having such a terrible time in the Bhagavad Gita. He doesn't want to fight those to whom he is attached. He does not want to give up. Even though the great issues of right or wrong and other moral factors are involved, he will not slay his kinfolk.

Krishna shows Arjuna that he must take a stand. Through fighting his kinfolk, he is not destroying them. He is transmuting them into love, into spiritual action, into spiritual realization, into awareness. But first he must give up the lower attachment to them.

This is a great challenge, a great lesson. The instructions that are given over and over again in the Bhagavad Gita are absolutely essential to learning the lessons of life. It is one of the great guides and great scriptures that have been given us.

In the consciousness of freedom and nonattachment, I do whatever I need to do with love, gratitude, joy, and blessing.

■

Superiority of the Self

They say that the senses are superior to the body. The mind is superior to the senses. Superior to the mind is the intellect. The Self is superior to the intellect. (Bhagavad Gita 3:42)

Is there anything more beautiful than this teaching? Is there anything more clear? Knowing that the Self is superior to the intellect helps us to understand the "chain of command." The senses are superior to the body, the mind is superior to the senses, but the intellect is superior to the mind, which is a tool of the intellect.

Our thinking, our comparing, our correlating, our categorizing—all of these are done with the mind, but superior to the mind is the intellect. However, there is something superior to the intellect, and that is the Self, which knows all and is all—the unmanifest One.

The senses, the body, the mind, and the human intellect are all part of the manifest nature of Spirit. But now, to understand and establish dominion and freedom, liberation and self-realization, we must go beyond the manifest state and through the evolutionary process, releasing all form into the unmanifest state, which is the ultimate phase of the evolutionary thrust before it starts over again with involutionary action.

These great lessons are in the Bhagavad Gita. It is remarkable. It is awe-inspiring. Avail yourself of it, because you will find that it will bear great rewards.

Transcending body, senses, mind, and intellect, I am completely identified with the superiority of the Self in all that I say and do.

■

Manifestation of the One

Whenever there is a decline of righteousness, and the rise of unrighteousness, then I manifest Myself. (Bhagavad Gita 4:7)

Ralph Waldo Emerson said, "Things refuse to be mismanaged for long." This is a sort of paraphrase of an ancient truth that says when things are not working out, when the Arjuna, or the lower self, is not moving toward realization—then the Christ, or the Infinite, manifests itself.

That truth is told allegorically in the Christian tradition as the coming of the Christ. It is taught today by the Masters of Wisdom of the Hierarchy, who have brought forth the concept of the return of the Christ, the concept that the Christ must reappear in human affairs. Whenever we become indifferent to our duties and responsibilities—to our understanding of Dharma, the purpose of life—then the Christ must come and manifest Itself to protect the virtuous, to destroy the wicked, and to reestablish the sense of duty and responsibility. Thus: "I manifest myself, age after age." "From everlasting unto everlasting, I am God."

"Love the Lord thy God, with all thine heart, with all thy soul, with all thy might." When we do so we are unified with the Supreme. We reach a state of consciousness from which there is no return. The knowledge of the Self dissolves all attachment.

I am free from all evil, error, and negativity. Everything in my life express-es good, as the Christ and the Infinite One are manifest within me.

■

Action and Inaction

He who in action recognizes inaction, and in inaction sees action, is a wise man. He is a Yogi and accomplishes all his work. (Bhagavad Gita 4:18)

What do we mean by action in nonaction and nonaction in action? This is a spiritual challenge. We must "judge not accord-ing to the appearance, but judge righteous judgment." For instance, we look at a solid rock and say, "This is solid and unmoving, there is no action here." But if we could look at it under a powerful microscope, we would find there is a great deal of molecular action going on there all the time. Nothing is static; there is action in everything. The yogi, the enlightened one, is able to see this action taking place everywhere, even though what happens is seeming nonaction.

Sometimes there is a great deal of outer action—for instance, the frenzy of a crowd or the turbulence of a storm. But at the center of the crowd or the storm, there is stillness. There is no action whatsoever. An Oriental proverb says, "All things are possible to him who can perfectly practice nonaction." In non-action, one becomes in union with the great Nonaction as well as the Action of the universe.

Does this mean we are eliminating our personal identity? No, it doesn't. It is a matter of dimension, of raising our conscious-ness to a higher level. When we become absorbed in the Divine—in the Supreme—we reach a state of Samadhi, of real-ization. From that point on, our identity is the identity of the One. We haven't lost our own identity. We have gained the iden-tity of the One.

I discern that action and inaction are energy polarities of right action, which is now taking place in my life on every level.

■

Freedom from Desire

He whose undertakings are free from desire and selfishness, and whose works are purified by wisdom, is an enlightened man. (Bhagavad Gita 4:19)

This reference is to one who has progressed along the path of self-realization, or one who is entering into the first stages of being a true yogi. So, we are counseled to act without desire or selfish purpose; further, whatever we do, we are to do it with wisdom.

Whatever we do, purposeful right action should be our commitment. If we are totally detached from the fruit of our action and from the action itself, we are ever content. We depend upon nothing. In so doing, though engaged in action, we are truly without action. We are poised and centered in the Universal Consciousness. We have detachment. We are free to proceed from the impetus of That which is within us, without trying to make things happen.

When Jesus says, "I and my Father are One," he refers to the state of being in which the little self is now no longer any part of what we are, because we are one with the One and we can declare, "Thy will be done." The Father's will is what is being done through us, because that is what our will is.

Primarily, the Bhagavad Gita comes from the Hindu tradition, but it is also universal. As with any universal spiritual teaching of Truth, it is limitless in its possibilities for interpretation, and we may require as much time as there is for us to come to a deeper understanding of it.

I am free from desire and selfishness, and all I do is purified by wisdom. The Light of the Spirit fills my consciousness.

Right Action

Having no desires, with the mind and self controlled, detached from all possessions, merely performing bodily action, he commits no wrong. (Bhagavad Gita 4:21)

Selflessness means to be centered in the Higher Self—not self-lessness by eliminating the Self, but in realizing the Self. A self-ish individual is one who is attached to the smaller self, the little, personal, human ego-self.

Upon becoming selfless, we have moved from the little self to the Higher Self. We do not let our possessions rule or own us. We act through the body, but see the body as an instrument, as a channel. We know that our body is the manifestation of Spirit and Intelligence and has no power over us, unless that power is given to it. A selfless individual sees things in their proper relationships.

The body must be conquered, but we ought not to think of this process as an external conquering. We conquer our body by conquering ourselves, by learning how to control our will.

We bring our senses under control. We align them with Truth, rather than appearance. When all of these things are done—acting with dedication, conquering the body, bringing the senses under control—we realize that our self is One with the Self of all beings. That signals the coming of wisdom, when we can do everything we are called upon to do.

My mind, body, and emotions are under control as I focus upon the perfection within me and express it in every way.

■

Freedom

Renunciation of action and unselfish performance of works both lead to liberation. But of the two, unselfish performance of works is superior to renunciation of action. (Bhagavad Gita 5:2)

Renunciation means not to do things—to withdraw completely and not express. But there is a preferable path, which involves the performance of action.

It is relatively easy, for instance, for a person to withdraw into a cave and have nothing to do with the things of the outer world. That is one way, but how about the person who is in the busy street, among the crowds, and finds realization there, too? The Teachers say this way is preferable. It is more practical and takes more discipline, and the rewards that come as a result are much greater.

As Emerson said, "Blessed is he who in the midst of the crowd can keep the serenity of his own solitude." That is the trick. The person who is withdrawn and is practicing renunciation completely is not confronted by the challenges of the outer world. Such a person has other challenges, but is not dealing with material reality.

If we are on the firing line, we are challenged all the time. But we are called upon, if we would be of any value in service or if we would grow spiritually, to keep that same renunciation of action while we are in the midst of the action.

Whatever I do, I do it unselfishly and with all my might, thereby attaining freedom and expressing love in every action.

■

Purification

He who works with purity of soul, who is master of his self, who has subdued his senses, who realizes his Self is the Self of all beings, even though he works, he is not tainted. (Bhagavad Gita 5:7)

Dedicated action is the way to purify your mind. Don't you feel good when you do worthwhile things—when you are dedicated to something, when you fulfill a difficult assignment or do a good job, or when you are doing something for somebody else?

That is when the purification comes, because you are doing it with the fire of enthusiasm, coupled with the elixir of love, and that purifies your mind. You always purify your mind when you forget about your little self. That is the purpose of meditation. Meditation is the time when we forget the little self and become immersed in the majesty and immensity of the Entire Self, and are purified as the result.

Purifying your mind through dedicated action helps you conquer your body. The body has many different ways of enslaving you. It gets hungry. It gets tired. It hurts. It has urges. It has desires. All of these are constructive in their way, but if they enslave you, then they detract from the Self.

But you are not bound or attached to results, to selfish concerns, or to anything else. You simply see your Entire Self as an instrument which is expressing the love that the Universal Self has for all selves of all the kingdoms, wherever they are.

As I subdue my senses, I am pure in my soul. I realize that my Self is the Self of all beings.

■

Knowledge

Directing your whole conscious being to the supreme, and concentrating solely on That, your sins are dispelled by knowledge and you reach a state from which there is no return. (Bhagavad Gita 5:17)

You are called upon to dedicate your intelligence to the Supreme, and whatever you go about, to see it in the Light of the Divine. "I bless you in the Light of the Divine. Be blessed by the Divine." When you focus your intelligence upon the Supreme, then you are absorbed by it. You actually lose your sense of personal little-self identity. You ask to be absorbed by the Self, and as you put your entire attention upon the Self, It will absorb you.

When you are involved in a project, you may feel completely absorbed in your work. Why? Because you have filled your mind, your soul, your action, and your awareness with the action you are engaged in.

This teaching says that there is a higher level of absorption than just absorbing yourself in sense gratification. Absorb yourself in action through the high Karma Yoga action of service, thereby absorbing yourself in the Higher Self. Then you are lifted up by It, and your purpose, your dedication, and your action become the action of the Divine. The entire Bhagavad Gita is directed at helping this to happen.

I dedicate my entire conscious being to the Supreme. As I concentrate solely upon the One, all error is dissolved and I am blessed.

The Eternal Goal

*Free from pride and delusion, victorious over the evil of attachment,
all desires stilled, ever devoted to the One, freed from the pairs of opposites such as pleasure and pain, the undeluded reach the Goal
Eternal. (Bhagavad Gita 15:5)*

In this state of attunement and alignment, we come to the powerful
concept that is brought out in all great spiritual teachings—the
state of Grace.

Paul, in the Bible, was able to experience this state very closely
when the Lord said unto him, *"My Grace is sufficient for thee."* (II
Corinthians 12:9)

Grace is the impersonal outpouring of God's Life into our being.
That is all there is to know and all you need to know to follow the
Way, the Path of Light, which moves ever onward, ever upward.
God's center is everywhere; His circumference is nowhere, and the
bottom line of all Spiritual Truth has not yet been written. True
Grace has not yet been achieved, but we keep moving on, spiraling
up the mountain toward the summit, where the One is waiting to
greet us, envelop us in Its Entire Being, and bring us into that state
of constant Inner Knowing—of Grace, Peace, Love.

When our little self—Arjuna, our younger, little, personal ego-
self—is in charge, we are often upset by things that take place in the
world. But when we align ourselves totally with the Higher Self, we
are lifted up from this world and are drawn to a higher level. The
battle is not an external battle at all; it is an inner one. When we

read the Bhagavad Gita and meditate upon it, we should do so with this idea in mind.

I am disciplined, dedicated, and devoted to the One. I am free from the pairs of opposites and I reach the Goal Eternal.

■

One with God

In this world everything is overcome by those whose minds are established in equality. God is flawless and the same in all. Therefore these persons are established in the One. (Bhagavad Gita 5:19)

Jesus said, "And I, if I be lifted up from the earth, will draw all men unto me." We are all joined together when we are following the One. We are fellow disciples in that way—fellow aspirants, devotees, chelahs—because we are not just pursuing goals or endeavors, or even group endeavors. We are realizing our oneness with the One, and that, of course, makes us united in unity.

There is an algebraic axiom which says, "Things that are equal to the same thing are equal to each other." Spiritual law would say that those who are dedicated to the same thing, who are dedicated to common purpose, are dedicated to each other. Therefore, they are one with each other.

Why should there be stress and strain? Why should we toil and endure needless suffering when we can go to the center and find there our oneness with the One, and find the peaceful, blissful unfoldment of our lives? As we practice meditation, we learn how to be still and to know that the Presence within is God.

In the Bhagavad Gita, Krishna, the Higher Self, is teaching Arjuna, our soul, which is continuing to grow. Krishna is the Teacher; Arjuna is the chelah. The setting is a battlefield, symbolic of the fact that our Higher Self and our lower self are often in conflict with each other and that the two together are building our consciousness.

I am transformed as my mind is unified and attuned to God, the Omnipotent Good. The world is overcome as I am established in the One.

■

Happiness

When the soul is no longer attached to external objects, happiness is found in the Self: Meditation upon the One brings eternal bliss. (Bhagavad Gita 5:21)

Dr. Ernest Holmes used to say, "Remember, compared to the reality of your own Self, all of these things out here are toys. Magnificent many of them, but toys nevertheless." Detach yourself from the external. With your release and detachment, the Self takes you into Its household, and you are one with the Self.

The pleasures that are the result of contacts, the things that happen, the things that we create, the things that are given to us, the things that come our way, our momentary good fortune—all of these appear and disappear. These contacts are really the source of sorrow. All outer things have a beginning and an end. Krishna, the Teacher, is telling us here, however, that Truth—Reality—has no beginning and no end.

Emerson says, "God will not allow his works to be made manifest by cowards." In other words, if you don't shape up, if you don't have discipline and develop yourself or conquer yourself, then God seems to be your enemy because you are punished by your own nothingness and you blame God for it and make an enemy of God. Children who are disciplined look upon their parents as enemies because their childish will is opposed. That is where we are. We are all children, aren't we? And Father-Mother God is as our parents.

As I meditate upon the One, my soul is freed from all external attachments, and I find happiness and bliss in the Self.

The Self

Let an individual lift himself by his own Self alone, and let him not lower himself. The Self alone is the friend of oneself, and the self alone is the enemy of oneself. (Bhagavad Gita 6:5)

Magnificent, if we just take the time to discern what it means. "Let an individual lift himself by his own Self alone." You have heard the old statement, "You can't lift yourself up by your own bootstraps." That is an everyday way of saying, "You can't lift yourself by yourself." In other words, if you want to be lifted up in your mind, your motives, and in your spiritual aspiration, then you must be lifted up by That which is above you. The wonderful old hymn "Love Lifted Me" declares, "Love lifted me. Love lifted me. When nothing else would help, Love lifted me."

You may be bogged down and unable to get anywhere, but when you have love, it lifts you. Let your Higher Self lift you. The Self alone is the friend of self. Your real friend is the Self, the One, the Infinite—Krishna, in this case. He is personifying the Infinite to Arjuna, who is the struggling soul. The self alone is its own enemy—our little personal ego, our little personality self. This is the enemy of ourselves. We are our own worst enemy, and we must align ourselves with That which is our true friend, the True Self.

The Self is the friend of the self for those who have conquered themselves through the Higher Self. But to the unconquered self, the little undisciplined and unrealized self that creates so much havoc and suffering, the Higher Self is an enemy.

The Self lifts me above my self. The Self is my eternal friend. I am filled with an all-embracing love which lifts me to the heights.

■

Love

He who is equal-minded among friends, enemies, the indifferent, the neutral, the hateful, the righteous and the unrighteous, he is superior. (Bhagavad Gita 6:9)

Now what does the Gita say that we need to do to become a superior person? *"Have equal regard for friends, enemies, the indifferent, the neutral, the hateful, the righteous and the unrighteous . . ."* What did Jesus say? *"Love your enemies, bless them that curse you, do good to them that hate you, pray for them which despitefully use you and persecute you"* (Matthew 5:44). We are to have equal regard for friends and enemies.

If enemies are setting themselves up to destroy you, to inconvenience you, or to do things against you, love them. Love them. "Release them lovingly into the hands of the Father." Bless them.

See them in the Light of the Divine and release them.

The same teaching applies to people who make a case against you, to those who are hateful. You are called upon to have as much regard for them as you do for your relatives, and as much regard for the sinner as you do for the saint. When you do that, you certainly will be a superior person. Not *if* you can do it, but *when* you do it.

Love and equal-mindedness are established as our only acceptable attitudes toward one another. The ability to act with equanimity rather than animosity is the mark of a superior person. All of us have the capacity to reach the level of consciousness where we are in control of our feelings and actions, and have dominion over all relationships.

As I forgive all, I am forgiven. In place of my old negative feelings, I give positive, constructive feelings of love and peace.

■

Peace

Try constantly to keep the mind steady, remain in solitude, with mind and body free from desires and possessions. (Bhagavad Gita 6:10)

We learn to affirm: "I am poised and centered in the Christ Consciousness and nothing can disturb the calm serenity of my soul." An Oriental aphorism states, "All things proceed from the quiet mind." Calm, quiet, peace, and silence are progressive stages of arriving at that inner state which we designate as "the Silence."

Both the Bible and the Bhagavad Gita declare the value of centering the mind in the inner, subjective realm, and freeing it from all objective, external concerns. The principle is one of release, of letting go, and letting God fill our entire being. God is our Real Self.

Krishna uses the personal pronoun "I" not as the expression of Himself as a personality, but of Himself as one with the One in the same way Jesus does when He says, *"I and my Father are One"* (John 10:30). Jesus and Krishna and the Christ are One. Jesus is the person. Christ is the Spirit embodied in the person. This is true of each one of us. *"Christ in you, the hope of glory"* (Colossians 1:27). Jesus says, in effect, "Once you meditate upon these things and identify with the One, then I supply you with whatever you do not possess— whatever you need, even though you don't know how to get it—if you know how to go to the Source and praise God from Whom all blessings flow."

The yogi is one who is unified with the Truth. Yoga is Oneness. A yogi is one who practices Oneness. We are all yogis when we are unified with spiritual Truth. Yoga itself is the science of the Spirit. The yogi is one who practices the art and the science of the Spirit.

Calm. Quiet. Peace. Silence. As I go to my inner place, my mind becomes steady and I am free from all outer influences.

■

Mind

Undoubtedly, the mind is difficult to control and restless, but it can be controlled by constant practice and detachment. Yoga is hard to attain by one who is not self-controlled, but is attainable through discipline. (Bhagavad Gita 6:35-36)

Let us remember that yoga means "union." What Krishna is saying here is that yoga is hard to attain by those who are not able to control themselves. So, we (as Arjuna) find ourselves asking, "How do I learn to control myself?" The answer is inevitable: "By yoga." "I attain yoga by yoga?" Obviously. The only way you can attain yoga is by practicing yoga. "Well, how can I practice yoga when I haven't yet attained yoga?"

You become still, you observe, and you ask yoga to tell you about itself, and it will tell you what it is. You will focus upon what it is, and as you focus upon what it is, the yoga—union—starts to take place. Therefore, you have attained a measure of yoga by practicing yoga.

You don't stand back and take refuge by saying, "My mind is hard to control" or "I get hungry" or "I get sleepy" or "I get interested in other things and my mind wanders." Krishna would say, as would any good teacher, "Okay, join the club. Those things happen to all of us."

However, they don't have to happen, because what you are after, and what you are doing in your yoga, is not playing the game of the restless, turbulent mind. You are aligning yourself with the Supreme, with the One. So, you can't really be "in union" if you can't control yourself. But you can control yourself by practicing control, by practicing that which is yoga. That is the path of right striving.

I am poised and centered in the Self. With the disciplines of detachment and constant practice, I achieve control over my mind.

■

Creation

God, the One, is the Supreme, higher than all else. His essential nature is the Self Action and work (Karma) is the creative force which brings beings into manifestation. (Bhagavad Gita 8:3)

What does it all mean? For us, the Bhagavad Gita is intensely personal, intensely practical. It gives us all the instruction we need, all the time we need to find spiritual guidance and to move toward Union with the One. This is what it is all about. This is the whole message and purpose of the Bhagavad Gita. The Imperishable is the Eternal One, the Supreme One. It dwells in the body and becomes the indwelling place. There is no place where it is not.

The action of the creative process is the Supreme Self, as Spirit, unfolding. Action is the creative process of the Supreme reuniting with Itself, as it has been on this far journey into human consciousness and into the human body and human manifestation.

Krishna frequently mentions the departure that is coming someday. We'll not always be here in this present tangible experience, no matter how dear our relationships and how permanent our attachments seem. The Bible says, *"For the former things are passed away... Behold I make all things new"* (Revelations 21:4, 5). A time of departure will come.

It has been said that the best instruction for living is to know how to meet that part of living which will entail our departure from the current scene. We can't use the words "death" and "dying" because those are delusions. It is only Eternal Life, going through different phases, different forms, different expressions.

The creative activity of the Infinite brings all good things into manifestation in my life. I am one with God, the Supreme, the Highest.

Being

> *My perishable nature is the basis of all created things—the objective phenomenon of being. The Cosmic Spirit (the subjective phenomenon of existence) is the basis of the divine elements.*
> *(Bhagavad Gita 8:4)*

The perishable, the objective, is always the outer. So the objective phenomena, the things that we see "out there," are the ones we respond to with our five senses. The Indweller is the subjective phenomenon. The subjective is inner. Subjective phenomena include love, peace, truth, harmony, intuition, awareness, inspiration, and all spiritual qualities.

How clear it is to see that the objective phenomenon is the tangible, the external. There can't be an inside without an outside or an outside without an inside. Krishna, the Eternal One, is objective, as we see in the rocks, the trees, and all things tangible and physical, including the mineral, animal, and vegetable kingdoms of nature as well as all of humanity. All things in outer form, the external, are perishable.

The Indweller is the subjective phenomenon of existence. It is always there. So, for each of us personally, the Eternal One is the Indweller. *"Neither shall they say, Lo here! or, Lo there! For behold, the kingdom of God is within you"* (Luke 17:21). That is the Indweller. The Bhagavad Gita teaches us how to dwell in the inner instead of the outer.

Jesus taught it by saying, *"Judge not according to the appearance, but judge righteous judgment"* (John 7:24). *"The kingdom of God is within you."* That is where the subjective reality is.

There is no place where God leaves off and I begin. The Father and I are One. There is only Perfect God, Perfect Person, Perfect Being.

■

Oneness

At all times remember Me. When thy mind and understanding are absorbed in Me, you will come to Me alone. (Bhagavad Gita 8:7)

The Bible commands, *"Thou shalt have no other gods before me"* (Exodus 20:3). The Bhagavad Gita demands ultimate and single focus: we must remember God "at all times." There is no other refuge and no other destination: ". . . you will come to Me alone."

The Law of Absorption is explained in both the Bible and the Bhagavad Gita as that state of complete Oneness when there is no place where God leaves off and we begin. We absorb each other. Until this takes place there is God and person, but when we "draw nigh to Him," He "draws nigh to us," absorbs us, and then there is only God, because God in us, as us, is us.

In meditation we reach the realization that there is only One. This is confirmed in the Bible: *"Even from everlasting to everlasting, thou art God"* (Psalm 90:2). This is all we really need to know.

There are fragments of this teaching scattered throughout the Christian Bible, even though the use of it has not yet fully been understood. Read the Sermon on the Mount: *"Consider the lilies of the field..."* (Matthew 6:28). What shall I eat? What shall I wear? *"Your heavenly Father knows you have need of all these things. Seek first the kingdom of God and his righteousness; and all these things shall be added unto you"* (Matthew 6:32, 33).

Since we are one with the One, we have complete protection and all we require to care for ourselves. Experiencing His Presence within us at all times, we discover no difference between the Real Self and our own Higher Self. "From everlasting unto everlasting," the God Presence is within us, and we are lifted up to expanded realization on all levels.

My mind, heart, and soul are absorbed into the One. In all my ways I acknowledge Him, and He directs my path.

■

Worship

Self-conceited, stubborn, filled with pride and arrogance of wealth, they perform sacrifices in name only, but of ostentation and with no regard for rules. (Bhagavad Gita 16:17)

In this passage, the Bhagavad Gita tackles our puffed-up personal ego problem. The passage is explicit in pointing out that external concerns and outer show have no place in our relationship with God. They are, as Shakespeare says, "full of sound and fury, signifying nothing."

Definite requirements and rules must be adhered to when we "perform sacrifices" (worship) and when we pray. These spiritual expressions require humility, simplicity, and purity of mind and motive.

The human self must be transcended by the Divine Self. Personality and possessions must be surrendered to the One. The instruction here is to get our priorities straight. Unless God comes first, nothing will be produced by our outer display. Nothing can come from nothing. Transcend your nothingness in true worship (i.e., making worthy).

The Bhagavad Gita leads us into thinking about the One and then into consciously becoming one with it. Think about the One, but then release your thought and let it join with the One. The One is everywhere. In the One, all beings are like the wind.

"Where is the snow of yesteryear?" Where has it gone? It is gone, but not gone. Coming and going. Returning again. All the time, whether coming or going, in manifestation or in unmanifestation, we are one with Him. One with the One.

All puffed up personal egotistical pride and arrogance are dissolved from my consciousness as I reach transcendence.

■

Life

I am the highest. I am the life in all existences. I am the external seed of all beings. All manifestations are born from me. (Bhagavad Gita 7:10-12)

We have learned to affirm: "There is One Presence and One Power in the Universe—God, the Good, Omnipotent, present and active in my life and in all of my affairs."

As sweeping and all-inclusive as this affirmation is, it is not an overstatement. It is absolute Truth. Not only is God in everything, God *is* everything. There is no opposing power. There is only One Power. The One is Omniscient, Omnipresent, Omnipotent, and Omniactive.

An ancient Greek philosopher, Empedocles, said, "God is that whose center is everywhere, and whose circumference is nowhere." Emerson said, "God is that which peoples the lonely places." The Bible says, *"Even from everlasting to everlasting, thou art God"* (Psalms 90:2).

Here, then, is what the Bhagavad Gita and other great scriptures and teachers say about God. What do *you* say about God? Whatever you say He is, that is what He is to you.

When we consciously think about anything, what we think about becomes real in our experience. So if we are thinking about God, thinking about the Eternal, thinking about love, thinking about service, thinking about sacrifice, thinking about offering of ourselves—we consciously become one with the One.

Emmet Fox perceived this when he affirmed: "I have conscious Divine Intelligence. I individualize Omniscience. I have direct knowledge of Truth. I have perfect Intuition. I have Spiritual Perception. I know."

My life is an expression of the Infinite Life which is the Source from which all things are born. I am a child of God.

■

Wisdom

He who seeks wisdom is established in me alone as the highest goal. (Bhagavad Gita 7:18)

In designating wisdom as the highest possible goal, the Bhagavad Gita is actually saying that wisdom is God-consciousness and is also telling what happens when we seek wisdom. We establish our consciousness on a high level by seeking wisdom; we are established in God when we seek wisdom, when we keep it as our supreme goal until we find it. The Bible likewise recognizes wisdom as the most important attainment of life. It unequivocally says to get wisdom.

Wisdom includes the balance and equilibrium that come from experience, from instruction, and from spiritual realization. These are the sources of wisdom. But as important as wisdom is, we cannot stop there. We must "keep on keeping on" until we get *understanding*. After wisdom comes understanding. Understanding is "standing under" God's Law—standing under the realization of that overall canopy of Light, Love, and Truth.

So get knowledge and information, then get wisdom. Know how to relate to yourself, how to relate to God, and how to relate to your world. This will give you understanding. Stand under Truth. Stand under the Law and the Presence of God.

All ignorance and foolishness are dissolved from my consciousness as I seek wisdom and understanding of Truth.

■

First Cause

> *All beings do not consciously dwell in Me, but I am the Cause of all beings. My Spirit sustains them. All existences abide in Me. (Bhagavad Gita 9:5,6)*

"All beings do not consciously dwell in Me." They do live in the One, but not consciously. The beings of the mineral kingdom, for instance, are beings: little life-things, little energy beings. They are alive but they don't live consciously in the Eternal Being.

Regarding the vegetable kingdom, Jesus says, "*Consider the lilies of the field, how they grow; they toil not, neither do they spin: and yet...even Solomon in all his glory was not arrayed like one of these*" (Matthew 6:28, 29). Flowers do not think consciously. They are content just to be, like the lilies of the field of which Jesus spoke.

In the animal kingdom, a fish is content to be a fish. Fish do not consciously know they live in the One, nor do those wonderful inhabitants of the animal kingdom, our domestic pets. They sometimes seem to think consciously, but they are actually expressing from their instinctive nature. They do not consciously know.

In the human kingdom, few people consciously remind themselves that they are one with God. They are unconsciously one with God. But when we think about it then we consciously know that we are one with the One. The Bhagavad Gita helps us to think consciously about it.

As all existences abide in the One, and I am One with the One, I am one with all the kingdoms of Nature and they are one with me.

∎

Forgiveness

He who has no ill will to any being, who is friendly and compassionate, free from egoism and attachment, balanced in pleasure and pain, patient and forgiving, and ever content, self-controlled, unshakable in determination, with mind and understanding dedicated to Me, he My devotee, is dear to Me. (Bhagavad Gita 12:13, 14)

How marvelous these teachings are—so impactful and complete. The instructions are almost identical with those given by the Christ: *"Love your enemies." "A new commandment I give unto you, That you love one another ... "*

"Tranquil in pleasure and pain," says Krishna. This is divine indifference. In "If," the poet Kipling says, "If you can meet with triumph and disaster, And treat those two impostors just the same..."

Krishna refers to being "full of forgiveness." (To forgive means to "give for"—exchange for the attitude that you have, new attitudes of Spirit and Light.) The Bible says: *"Draw nigh to God, and He will draw nigh to you"* (James 4:8). *"In all thy ways acknowledge Him, and He shall direct thy paths"* (Proverbs 3:6). Paul, in the Bible, says, *"I have learned, in whatsoever state I am, therewith to be content"* (Philippians 4:11).

That is what Krishna is talking about—the state of having learned to control your body, mind, and senses. You are in charge of your body, your mind, and your senses. *"There is self-determination."* Keep your eye on the goal. *"Who has dedicated his heart and mind to Me."* Practice dedication, devotion, and discipline. Then you are a devotee and you are dear to the Master.

Friendly and compassionate, balanced in pleasure and pain, patient and forgiving, I trust in the Lord with all my heart.

The Creative Process

At the coming of day, all manifested things come forth from the unmanifested, and at the coming of night all manifestation returns to the Unmanifested One. (Bhagavad Gita 8:18)

Dawn is the birth; Evening is the departure. The Creative Process is from Day (Dawn) into Night (Evening). This is also the process of involution and evolution. This action starts with the Day. All manifestation proceeds from the Unmanifested One. Spirit (Energy) proceeds downward and becomes manifest. This is the process of involution, when the Spirit becomes manifest. Then the process starts moving back upward to the Unmanifest. It started from the Unmanifest, it becomes manifest and then proceeds back to the Unmanifest, whence it started.

The instruction here is for us to remember that Creative Process, that process of creative action. Once the thrust of the involutionary energies of Spirit is put into form, then we need this instruction of the Bhagavad Gita, this instruction of the yogis, this instruction of Yoga, this instruction of Krishna, to free ourselves from form. We do so progressively during our entire conscious life when we are on the Path.

We don't say, "I am preparing to die." No, we say, "I am living fully because I am freeing myself from the external form, from the limitations of my thought. I am freeing myself from that, and so when I reach the Ultimate Freedom, the last thing I free myself from is my consciousness." When you are free from that, then, as Gibran says in *The Prophet,* "shall you truly dance."

As the perfection of the Infinite descends into my being, I evolve into the full and perfect expression of God's wholeness.

■

Security

Those who worship Me, and meditate on Me alone, I bring attainment for what they have not, and security for what they already possess. (Bhagavad Gita 9:22)

These supernal passages need no interpretation, explanation, or description when we align ourselves with them. The One can be in multitudinous external manifestations, but it is not depleted. The whole is greater than the sum of all of its parts. This seems mathematically impossible, but it is true. It is the Eternal Spiritual Law.

Actually, action in service is a form of meditation. It is one way of attaining serenity and peace. When we attain Union with the Self—whether through inaction or through action, however we reach that Union—serenity is with us from that point on.

This doesn't mean that we stop action, but that serenity is the quality of our action.

So, just by the very nature of Being, there is action. The teaching is to learn to rise above action into the consciousness of inaction. But in inaction, there is also action. An Oriental proverb says, "All things are possible to him who can perfectly practice nonaction." Or, you can seek to "become poised and centered in the Christ consciousness, and know that nothing can disturb the calm serenity of your soul," which is a modern metaphysical paraphrasing of this Ancient Truth.

I am safe and secure in the everlasting arms of my "Father which is in heaven," Who is the substance and the essence of all that I am and all that I have.

■

Part VI

West Meets East through the Three Gunas

The Yoga of the Three Modes: The Gunas

Sattva, Rajas, Tamas, the three gunas, are born of Nature and bind the True Self to the body. (Bhagavad Gita 14:5)

The three gunas are the impulses born of Nature and are active in every aspect of Life. The gunas, which are inherent in all manifestation and expression, in all action and reaction, are the three levels of consciousness on both the universal and the individual levels. They are both the substance and the process governing all phenomena.

The gunas are the way Life works in its subjective state; everything and all people are in bondage to Natural Law until they transcend it by establishing dominion over it. Inherent in the created is the potential of Oneness with the Creator. When this union is attained, the created can consciously use the Laws of Nature (the gunas) to assist in its evolutionary pathway toward perfection. The three qualities of Nature—Sattva (goodness), Rajas (passion), and Tamas (ignorance)—are three levels of consciousness, and condition the soul of the individual.

> *There is no being on earth or in heaven who is free from the conditioning of the three gunas. (Bhagavad Gita 18:40)*

In explaining the power of the gunas to determine the experience and the evolution of the individual soul, the Bhagavad Gita gives us a basic spiritual psychology which enables us to meet the challenges of life and fulfill our purpose. When we understand the gunas and learn to work with these levels of consciousness, we free ourselves from limitation and negative conditioning, and we move toward the attainment of our full potental.

Understanding the gunas is essential if we are to grasp the central teaching of the Gita: we are divine expressions of the One, but can only express complete Oneness by understanding our natural components and tendencies. This is basic psychology, and is the precursor of modern Western psychological approaches. In this way modern West meets ancient East, making progress in helping the individual understand the mystery of life.

Sattva

Sattva, goodness and purity, gives health and understanding, but it binds the Higher Self by attachment to happiness and knowledge. (Bhagavad Gita 14:6)

The Sattvic consciousness of higher awareness and illumined understanding lifts us to the realization of our spiritual nature and raises the quality of our life. Sattva elevates us to the highest possible level as a human being. However, even the highest human and worldly attainment is bondage to the Spiritual Self. No matter how happy we may be and how much enlightenment we may attain, these worldly states are a limitation to That which is unlimited. Happiness and joy fall short of the spiritual state of bliss which comes when we transcend the three modes of experience (the gunas) and dwell in the Absolute—the state of Oneness with the One.

The Bhagavad Gita shows us that our temporal states, governed by the gunas, are transitory, while our spiritual essence is eternal. The spiritual psychology that Krishna teaches Arjuna is not concerned with the human being; its focus is upon the spiritual being. This original spiritual psychology deals with the true meaning of the word—"psychology"—knowledge of the soul. Modern Western psychology tends to limit its attention to the mental and emotional aspects of consciousness, largely ignoring the vast realm of the spiritual.

However, West is meeting East as both evolve toward a greater realization of our spiritual nature. Western psychologists are developing more spiritual awareness, while Eastern spiritual psychology is becoming more practical in dealing with the everyday issues of life. There is emerging an all-embracing, balanced approach which deals with the whole person. Only now are we beginning to see that the Bhagavad Gita has taught this for thousands of years.

The Bhagavad Gita is multidimensional, giving detailed information and instruction about each of the three gunas and That which lies beyond them.

Sattvic Characteristics and Qualities

Sattva is the upper level of human consciousness, and is characterized by radiance, purity, goodness, joy, and light. Health, knowledge, wisdom, and understanding are the result. Self-control, purity of motive, and serenity of mind characterize the Sattvic individual, who also tends to be gentle, kind, loving, responsible, generous, and devoted to duty. The Sattvic person is in tune with the rhythm of the Universe and experiences and demonstrates law, order, right action, right place, and right timing.

Obviously, Sattva is a highly desirable state of near perfection, but it is nevertheless one of the gunas and must be transcended. However, this is a matter of evolution rather than effort. Through discipline, dedication, and devotion, the aspirant moves from the lower level of Tamas, through the middle level of Rajas, to the higher level of Sattva. It is a matter of self-unfoldment, attained by an expanding awareness of the Higher Self. Through spiritual disciplines, the aspirant establishes dominion over the individual human nature and experiences the freedom of Self-realization.

When we realize that we are in the world but not of it, we are no longer limited and enslaved by the gunas. We take up residence in a higher realm which transcends the gunas. We know the Truth and the Truth makes us free.

We unfold through progressive steps of experience, education, psychological instruction, therapy, and spiritual disciplines, as we evolve through many lifetimes.[4] The imprints of

---

[4]*Reincarnation has always been inherent in the Eastern teachings and is becoming increasingly accepted in the West.*

each of the gunas are deep-seated, and must be dissolved and their energies transmuted to higher vibrations of creative action. We are natives of eternity, and rising above the gunas by progressive steps is the initiating process by which we evolve into our true estate. This comes after we have attained total Sattva.

In Sattva we become aware of our oneness with the One. Beyond Sattva, we become One with the One. A grasp of this entire sequence of evolution is the dynamic which motivates and moves us through the gunas and beyond.

Rajas

Rajas is the nature of passion, springing from desire, greed, and attachment to action, which bind the embodied one. (Bhagavad Gita 14:7)

Rajas is the middle guna between Tamas and Sattva. In the Rajas consciousness we come to grips with the facts, appearances, and conditions of human existence. We have awakened from the inertia, darkness, and ignorance of Tamas, the primal lower level, but we have only a dim awareness of the higher levels of our potential which beckon to us from Sattva. We are grateful for our superiority over Tamas, but since we have an instinctive awareness of how far we have to go, we are filled with unrest and often indiscriminate activity. We know there is much to be done, but we don't know exactly what it is or how to go about it. We need all the assistance we can get to help us out of the human predicament in which we find ourselves.

In many ways, Rajas is the most challenging of the three gunas. In Tamas we are still asleep, in Sattva we can glimpse liberation, but in Rajas, we are deeply immersed in all the forces and expressions of both universal and individual nature. We fight against slipping back to Tamas, and we struggle to attain Sattva, but are not yet equipped to do so.

Rajas is filled with trial and error. Everything we encounter is a growth experience. Emotional and materialistic drives are strong, the mind is often confused, and our spiritual nature awakens only sporadically. We are pulled in many different directions as we plunge into action, trying to make the best of the situation. We are subject to many failures, but we are often victorious and achieve mighty works. The great need is for maturity, balance, and stability. Understanding Rajas factors allows us to attain and maintain these attributes.

Rajas Characteristics and Qualities

Rajas is the middle level of human consciousness and is characterized by passion, pride, desire, attachment, and effort. The

Rajassic individual is motivated by a need to do something about everything, and thus is governed by action. He or she feels very deeply about things, and is filled with a longing and thirst for more meaningful experience.

In this quest, the Rajassic individual develops strong appetites and is often greedy and selfish, and proud of his or her achievements. And with good reason. Many of the world's greatest achievements have been produced by Rajassic men and women—the leaders, the innovators; the empire builders; the captains of commerce, trade, and industry; the conquerors; and the rulers.

Rajas is a level that every individual and the world must go through on the path of unfoldment. It is the materialistic realm, and breeds attachment, pain, and sorrow as the result of unbridled ambition, self-aggrandizement, and rampant egotism. Rajas is a trap. The Rajassic individual is a necessary component in humanity's evolution, but the great abilities and tremendous energies of Rajas must be directed toward constructive purpose. The Rajassic individual must learn to love, to serve, and to work for the good of all, and the glory of the One.

It is in the vast field of Rajas that the transcendent message of the Gita makes its greatest impact. It is here that the modern West must call upon the wisdom and mysticism of the ancient East. The rampant Rajas of the modern world, still contaminated with the vestiges of our Tamassic origins, must somehow find the Sattvic light and move toward higher goals.

This is where the fields of spiritual philosophy, education, and psychology must meet the areas of materialistic scientific, mechanical, and computerized society, to work together to assist the evolution of all of humanity as spiritual beings. The world is the field where this is to take place. This is where West must meet East, forming a partnership dedicated to building and maintaining the kingdom of God on earth.

In order to completely understand our Rajassic stage we must take a look at how we got this way through Tamas.

Tamas

Tamas, born of ignorance and dullness, deludes all embodied beings, and binds them by negligence, indolence, and sleep. (Bhagavad Gita 14:8)

Tamas, the lowest of the three gunas, is the state of existence at the nadir of the involutionary thrust. When Spirit descends through substance and matter and takes form, it is completely embondaged until Spirit is reenergized and starts its evolutionary path upward. Tamas is the low level of consciousness, universally and individually, before Spirit awakens and moves upward. This is constantly taking place throughout Nature.

Tamas is the level connecting involution and evolution. It is the starting point for conscious cooperation with Spirit. This cooperation occurs automatically throughout Nature, subjectively in the three lower kingdoms—mineral, vegetable, and animal—but objectively and consciously in the human kingdom. The three lower kingdoms are under the dominion of the three gunas, but human beings have the potential to evolve beyond the gunas while at the same time recognizing and cooperating with them. This is because the human being has self-consciousness and therefore self-determination.

The human being moves upward through the three gunas both subjectively and consciously. The lower kingdoms are limited to the subjective nature of the gunas. For instance, the seed falls into the ground, sprouts, and sends forth its leaves. This is Tamas. The plant then experiences growth during which the buds appear. This is Rajas. The third stage is Sattva, when the blossoms and the fruit appear as the cycle of the three gunas is completed and the process begins over again. This is repeated endlessly without change or evolutionary progression. The plant is limited by the gunas.

The self-conscious human being, on the other hand, while subject to the three gunas, is not limited by these states of manifestation, and has the capacity to transcend them. However, there is nothing automatic about this. The individual must want to develop and grow. If incentive and desire are present, the individual will evolve progressively through the three gunas and beyond. If there is no incentive, the individual will languish in Tamas without evolving.

Tamas is the starting point. We can use it to launch ourselves into orbit, or we can remain there forever. The choice is ours. In order to learn what we are dealing with and how to make this choice intelligently, we must examine the Tamas characteristics and qualities.

Tamas Characteristics and Qualities

Everything and everyone starts from Tamas. It is the materialistic realm of the senses. The higher qualities are dormant when we remain in Tamas. Some individuals have never emerged from this primitive level. There are Tamassic Neanderthal men and women among us today—individuals who never evolved, and who are more animal than human. They have not exercised their freedom of choice to transcend the gunas by personal initiative.

Ignorance, inertia, and indolence are aspects of Tamas. Delusion, stupidity, and darkness characterize Tamassic individuals. They are not awake. They are conscious, but they are not aware. They lack discrimination and have no sense of values. Their appetites are bestial and sensual, with a tendency toward degeneracy and violence. The constructive qualities of Rajas have not yet emerged, and the admirable aspects of Sattva are completely unknown. Heedlessness and destructiveness are rampant, and those on the Tamassic level wander aimlessly in their moral and spiritual blindness.

Tamas is contagious and contaminates the entire human race, pulling it down into morasses of disease, crime, violence, war, starvation, suffering, and despair.

Turning its energies upward to assist spiritual evolution, Tamas is the beginning of civilization. As the energies turn downward and backward through indifference and neglect, Tamas brings about the end of civilization. It happened before in Atlantis and in the dark ages during and after the fall of Rome, and it is happening today. The forces of Tamas are active throughout the world. Humanity must endeavor to change direction and move upward, away from Tamas, through Rajas, Sattva, and beyond.

The gunas are aspects of creation, implanted in consciousness to assist the process of evolution by giving us the vision, the desire, and the opportunity to unfold into our full spiritual potential. The Bhagavad Gita shows us how to transcend the gunas, free ourselves from bondage, and move onward and upward toward Oneness with the One. All three gunas are active within humanity as a whole, and through each individual, all of the time. Life is a never-ending process of learning, growing, and evolving. The three gunas help us identify where we are on the path of evolutionary unfoldment.

As East and West join together in bringing about the marriage of Ancient Wisdom with modern technology, we help each other transcend the gunas and join together in Oneness with the One. The Bhagavad Gita helps West meet East in the experience and the realization that we are One with each other.

The Character of the One
Who Is Beyond the Three Modes

Arjuna said:

By what marks is he, O Lord, who has risen above the three modes characterized? What is his way of life? How does he get beyond the three modes?

The Blessed Lord said:

He, Arjuna, who does not abhor illumination, activity and delusion when they arise nor longs for them when they cease.

The individual who is seated like one unconcerned, unperturbed by the modes, who stands apart, without wavering, knowing that it is only the modes that act...

The person who regards pain and pleasure alike, who dwells in his or her own self, who looks upon a clod, a stone, a piece of gold as of equal worth, who remains the same amidst the pleasant and the unpleasant things, who is firm of mind, who regards both blame and praise as one...

One who is the same in honor and dishonor and the same to friends and foes, and who has given up all initiative of action, is said to have risen above the modes.

He who serves Me with unfailing devotion of love, rises above the three modes, he becomes eligible to attain the Eternal Abode. Bhagavad Gita (14:21-26)[5]

---

[5] *The Bhagavad Gita, With an Introductory Essay. Sanskrit Text, English Translation and Notes by S. Radhakrishnan, 1963, George Allen & Unwin Ltd., London, pages 323-324.*

Epilogue

*I*n this brief encounter with the salient teachings of the Bhagavad Gita we are sharing the universal Truths of spiritual understanding available to all of us.

East and West, North and South, join together in an inseparable unity of spiritual Oneness. There is a Golden Thread which runs through all spiritual teachings and is common to all of us.

We need to keep an open mind and to avail ourselves of the wonderful opportunities to learn from one another when we weigh and consider the blessings that pour out to us, as together we are Understanding and Standing Under the Bhagavad Gita.

Science of Mind
It Will Change Your Life

About the author:

The author of 30 best-selling books, **Dr. Donald Curtis** is a popular writer and teacher in the areas of spirituality, self-improvement, and metaphysics. He has appeared frequently on radio and television programs, including "The Oprah Winfrey Show," where he discussed "The True Meaning of the New Age."

Dr. Curtis has served as a minister of Religious Science and also of Unity. Prior to entering the ministry, he was a featured actor in more than 200 films produced by Hollywood's most famous studios. Dr. Curtis will be remembered for playing a starring role, "Mered," in Cecil B. DeMille's *The Ten Commandments*.

He now devotes his time to writing and lecturing.

For a list of books by Ernest Holmes, call 1-800-382-6121. Visit Science of Mind Online at http://www.scienceofmind.com.

The award-winning Science of Mind *magazine presents insightful and uplifting articles, interviews, and Daily Guides for Richer Living each month. For more information, call 1-800-247-6463.*

Science of **Mind** ®
A philosophy, a faith, a way of life